Journey Overcame

EVANGELIST LILLY RAY

authorHOUSE®

AuthorHouse™
1663 Liberty Drive
Bloomington, IN 47403
www.authorhouse.com
Phone: 833-262-8899

Published by AuthorHouse 07/08/2022

ISBN: 978-1-6655-6456-4 (sc)
ISBN: 978-1-6655-6455-7 (e)

Print information available on the last page.

Scripture quotations marked KJV are from the Holy Bible, King James Version (Authorized Version). First published in 1611. Quoted from the KJV Classic Reference Bible, Copyright © 1983 by The Zondervan Corporation.

This book is printed on acid-free paper.

ABOUT THE AUTHOR

Evangelist Lilly Ray is a women
of word a loving wife and mother
spreading the gospel of Jesus Christ.

DEDICATION

To

My husband James, my granddaughter, my three grandson Devante, Rytez, Jadarrius, great grandson Braydon, great granddaughter Lauryn, Nita and friends Carlene Ellis, William Holman, Curtis (Peter)Holman a good a good friend.

CONTENTS

INTRODUCTION

This is a story of my life as an evangelist. Whatever God call you to do, do it. Thanks God who allowed me to write this book "The Life of An Evangelist"

THE LIFE OF AN EVANGELIST

IN JULY 1999, I ACCEPTED my calling. At first, I didn't want to go, because being a woman, I was afraid of people. God said to preach his word and that is what I said that I would do, even if I have to preach it to the streets. Some people don't like female preachers in their pulpit. I always say, "If it's their pulpit and not God's I don't want any part of it anyways." 2nd Timothy 4:2 says, "preach the words; be instant in season and out of season."

We must preach, even when some people don't want to hear it. God's word must be

carried. How can people understand the word of God without a preacher? How can a preacher speak the word of God without having been sent by the beholder? We as preacher must do our job and trust in the lord for our increase. Ask God to anoint you. He can, and will, equip you for the word. We can't worry about what man says, because they don't have a heaven or a hell to puts us in. it is up to the beholder. We must do God work because his work must be done no matter what. We don't have any time to play around. We must be about our father's business. People should work while its day, because no man can work when night come.

In order to work for the lord, we must pick up our cross and follow him daily. This is a daily walk. We can't just work one day and stop. Some of us believe in only what we see, but the bible says that if we have faith of a grain of mustard seed, it can move mountains. By faith we understand that the world was formed by the word of God so that the things that are seen

were not made of things, which were visible. I am striving for what God has for me and wat he want me to do. It's not easy at first, but when you let God have his way in your life, everything will be all right. In order for a woman minister to preach, she must be determined, motivated and faithful to her work, because some of us will let man turn us around (which will not be a good thing).

Since I've been in the ministry I've had a few men to help me out: my brother-in-law has been a good influence in my life, as a minster, he has helped me with things that I didn't understand. He gave me books and commentaries of the bible. I thank God for him, because he is a pillar to our community. Also, my son and daughter's pastor has been a great help to me. He has let me preach at his church more than others. I thank God for him, another pastor who was there for me at the beginning. I was licensed and ordained at his church. He is a great man of God. He lets women preachers

preach at his church all the time. He is great in the word. I grew a lot under his leadership. He is an anointed man of God.

Also, another bishop has been a great inspiration in my life. He keep encouraging me in the world, he always prays with me about my problems. There is another pastor who helps me lots. He prays with me also. All their wives are ministers in the Gospel, and they are great too. My pastor is also a greatly anointed man of God. He is a good pastor. We've only had him for a year, but I can see the difference in the church. There was also a young woman who help me a lot. She is a very special lady. She talks big, but she will help you any way she can!!! She help me get everything that I needed when I moved back home. She runs a daycare. The children are blessed to have her in their lives. Gives God the praise for my sisters and brothers. Thanks to my sister in Christ. We work together to share the word of God with everyone. Thanks also go out to my other two friends whom both are working

for the lord and are being ever so faithful to God. Keep working for the lord. I thank God for each and every one of you. I would like to ask for God's blessing upon you all.

Special thank goes out to my husband. Thank God for my granddaughter. She has help me a whole lots, but she is not where she needs to be in the lord. I pray that she will soon arrives at that point in life. This is something that I have always wanted to do, write. I also want to write songs. I have written a few, but I haven't had them published yet. Seek God fist in your life. You cannot survive without him. We can do anything that we want to do as long as we have King Jesus

I have been tempted to write a book for a very long time, but I never have until now. It seems as if God will always let you know when it's time to work for him. Never let people push you into doing something that you know God is displeased with. It is time to thank God because he is an on time God, yes he is. To all

women and me whom God has called to preach, don't let anyone turn you around. Be patient and wait on him. We need to let him guide us instead of trying to guide ourselves. God is my guiding light in the time of darkness. We are all his children; therefore, we shouldn't have to walk in the darkness. There are so many people that are walking in the darkness. 1st John 1:15, this is the message that we have heard, and declare that God is light and in him there is no darkness at all.

To walk in the darkness mean to live to the moral character of God. You should never walk in the darkness.

It is time to get our house in order, because we don't know the day, time, or hour. So it's best to be ready at all times. You don't want him to come and catch you with your work undone. Matt 13:32, but have that day and hour, no one knows, not even the angels in heaven, or the son but the father. So we must get business affairs in order. There should be no more playing around.

We need to get serious about God's business. We have been dragging around too long. We're here to get God's good news spread.

The bible says, "We know the tree by the fruit it bears." We must carry the word of God and bear his fruit. We cannot plant apple and expect preaches to row.

Let us put in action: good. Not evil. Let's get out and spread the good news. Acts 10:38 says, "How God anointed Jesus of Nazareth with the holy spirit and with the power, who went about doing good and healing all who were oppressed by the devil. For God was with him." He's also with us today. We must work while its day; because when night comes we cannot work. So get busy spreading the gospel of Jesus Christ!!!!!!

BE LED BY GOD

Therefore we must have to please God; Hebrew 11:6; but without faith it is impossible to please God must believe that he is, and that he is a rewarder of those who diligently seek him. We must have faith and trust God. Put in action. I got saved at age ten. I've always have a desire to read the bible and sing although I have not always been as bold as I am now. But when you let God have his way in your life he will takes away all of your sins.

I know that God can do all things, and we can do all thig through Christ who strengthens us. With God in my life things are so different. For those of you all who don't have God in your

lives: get to know him!!!! Invite him in your lives Romans 10:9 says, "If you confess with your mouth and believe in your heart that God had raised Jesus up from dead, you will be saved". Then we became new. Men are done with the things that you used to do, and you know it is wrong and that you shouldn't do them anymore.

2nd Corinthians 5:17 says, "Therefore, if anyone is in Christ he is new creation, old things have passed away. Behold, all thing have become new." Our lives should change because we have been transformed into the likeness of Christ. 2nd Corinthians 3:18 says, "but we all with open face beholding as in a glass the glory of the Lord, are changed in the same image from glory to glory, even as by the spirit of the lord." God makes the difference in one life when you are born again. You just can't do any of the old things you please. You are new and are being led by the lord. Jon 14:26, "but the helper, the Holy Spirit whom the father will send in my name, he will teach you all things ad bring all things

to your remembrance. Whatsoever I have said unto you".

God is an awesome God. He can keep us out of trouble if we only look to him for help, because all of our help comes from him. Let him lead and guide you in the right path. Psalms 23:3 says, "He restoreth my soul, he leadeth me in the paths of righteousness. For the names sake." I am learning to let God direct my path to walk in the path of righteousness, because God knows the way of the righteousness. The ungodly shall perish', says psalms 1:6. We must be regenerated; this refers to the spiritual change brought about in our lives by the Holy Spirt. Normally in life, the change is from spiritual death to spiritual life. Which path will you choose???? I advise you to take the path of righteousness. That is the only way you can bear good fruit. The fruit of the spirit is love, peace, longsuffering, kindness, godliness and faithfulness. We should know how to live and bring about good fruit. Let peace abide in your

life when we were yet sinners, Jesus died for our sins on the cross at Calvary. We ought to bear good fruits for him and spread the good news everywhere we go: even when people don't want to hear you!!!!! Just keep spreading the good news of Jesus Christ.

Love your enemies. No one has seen God at any time. If we love one another, God will abide in us. 1st John 4:20 say, "If anyone says that they love God and they hate their neighbor, he is a liar. For he who does not love his brother does not love God. He who does not love his brother, whom he has seen, how can he love God whom he has not seen???

I JUST WANT MY SHARE

THE HARVEST IS TRULY PLENTIFUL, but the laborers are few (Matt 9:37). I just want my share of the work for the lord that started the plentiful harvest which is few in laborers. Stop grumbling, and start working. God want us to work together for him. Psalms 104:23 says, "Man goeth forth unto his work and to his labour until the evening". I remember when I was a child and we used to pray from sunrise to sunset. Sometimes, we used to chop cotton until the sun went down and if we can work for man like that then what is the problem when our savior ask f or us to work for him? There will be great benefits. We are supposed to make

labor in the gospel and not let the devil steal our joy. Don't let him tempt you with his tricks and schemes. Only you can prevent being an object of is torture, because he will use everything he can, including family, to try and keep you from doing the lord's work. He can even work through your body at times when we know it not right. Although, we do have choices to whether we do right and wrong because we know the difference between the two. I want and need my joy. Only through Jesus Christ can we do all things. Keep in mind that God will not force you into doing his work. He will let you decide for yourself.

The lord will never leave you nor forsake you. Even when your own family turns their backs on you he will always be there. Honestly, God is the only one you can depend on, because man will tell you one thing and do another. No president, governor, congressman, or senator can make you a promise and keep it. These are

just titles that we give people here on earth, but their honesty and loyalty is not guaranteed.

Psalm 128:2 says. "For thou shall eat the labour of thine hand; happy shalt thou be, and it shall be with thee". For example, if you have a garden and you plant seed but never plow them then it won't grow. It's the same exact way with the lord's work. If we say we are going to do things like go out and preach the word of the lord but don't do it then we will get no rewards. On the other hand, don't hesitate to work for man but psalms 127:1 says, "Except the lord build the house, the labour in vain that built it". So let's not let our work be in vain. Let us proclaim the gospel in Jesus Christ and carry the word with us wherever we go and share it with the unknowing. No matter where you are, never be ashamed to spread the word of God and let people know what he has done or you. I just want my share. We all have a job to do so let's get it! Get up and study so you can learn more about the lord our God. The lord

is counting on us to encourage the unsaved to become saved. We shouldn't let him down.

1st Timothy 5:17; 18 says, "Let the elders that rule well be counted worthy of double honour, especially they who labour in the word and doctrine. For the scripture saith, thou shalt not muzzle the ox that there threadeth the corn. And the labourer is worthy of his reward". We are not supposed to get the knowledge and not share it. We must share it with others, and the more we work, the better thing will be. Acts 20:35 says. "I have shewed you of all things, how that so laboring ye ought to support the weak, and to remember the words of the lord Jesus how he said, it is more blessed to give than to receive". There are those of us that are very weak in the flesh and in the spirt, and we are Christians see these people everyday and we don't do anything about it. God is not pleased with this. We are all serving one God who is above all, and everything we receive come from him so we should give him all we can by going

out and spreading the word that he is worthy to be praised.

Ephesians 4:7:11 says "But unto everyone of us is given grace according to the measure of the gift of Christ. And he gave some apostle; some prophets; some evangelist; some pastors; some teachers". We all have something to do for the up-building of the kingdom. We must put on the whole armour of God that ye may be able to stand against the trials of the devil. He will come after you when he sees you trying to do the will of God there is room for everyone to work stop pretending to be serious and actually get out there and be about the Lord business. Don't just put on a show for man, praise him. He is worthy to be praised with all your might. Let's all get our share of the blessing by doing what God expects of us.

Matt 11:28-30 say, "Come unto me, all ye that labour and are heavy laden and I will give you rest. Take my yoke upon you, and learn of me; for I am meek and lowly in heart; and ye

shall find rest unto your souls. For my yoke is easy, and my burden is light". A heavy laden may be burden with bills, sin, and other burdens. Jesus can take all or burdens away, because he promised to keep us and that we shall find us rest unto our souls. So you see, God can take all our burdens and do always with them. That's one of the many reason Satan doesn't want us to keep God in our hearts, another reason is because he know there will be absolutely no room for him to even think about coming in. if any creaks are left open the devil will try his best to come in and destroy you. We should all do the Lord's work to receive his blessing. I just want my share.

Printed in the United States
by Baker & Taylor Publisher Services